Alta H Haffner

Copyright: Alta H Haffner 2024
Email: alta@sakurabookpublishing.com
Sakura Book Publishing, Durban, South Africa
www.sakurabookpublishing.com

Title: The Haiku Collection

ISBN: 978-1-0370-1733-9(print)

978-1-0370-1734-6(e-book)

All rights reserved. No part of this publication may be reproduced, distributed, or transmitted in any form or any means, including photocopying, recordings, or other electronic or mechanical methods without the prior written permission of the author, except in the case of brief quotations embodied in critical reviews and certain noncommercial uses permitted by copyright law.

A Sky Full of Haiku

Tiny little stars
tucked inside an ancient language,
words that breathe within,
from season to season,
each syllable
a fingerprint pressed into time.

the cicadas scream for summer,
voices echo in my chest.

A heartbeat matched by the
pulse of this earth
reminding me that we are one...

Just dust
scattered beneath the blue sky,
painted with a million
Haiku verses.

About this Book

From the gentle morning light to the stillness at dusk...

This is a blend of traditional and modern Haiku and Tanka. Delicate imagery of cherry blossoms, dandelions, starry nights, melancholy moments and the tranquility of walking in a Japanese garden.

About the author

Alta H Haffner

Alta H. Haffner is a Haiku poet whose work captures the essence of precious, fleeting moments with simplicity and depth. Born with a deep appreciation for the beauty of brevity, Alta's Haiku poems reflect her keen observation of nature and her ability to evoke emotions in just a few short lines.

Drawing inspiration from the ever changing seasons, the delicate balance of the natural world, and the quiet whispers of every new dawn, Alta's Haiku poems invite readers to slow down, pause, and appreciate the present moment. With a handful of syllables, she allows her readers to contemplate.

Through her Haiku poetry, Alta H. Haffner reminds us of the beauty that can be found in simplicity, the power of mindfulness, and the importance of being fully present in each moment.

your inner beauty
reflecting a sunny day
in midst of winter

do you remember
a touch silky soft and warm
leaning against thorns

strength of a woman
tears turned to titanium
rise to a new morn'

our misguided trust
such painful disappointments
truth hidden rainbow

lonely starry nights
forgotten promise at night
the sun beaming bright

my evergreen view
I cried a river of tears
you held icy snow

touch my scarlet lips
a sorrowful encounter
red spider lily

a gust of ume
japanese garden of hope
our sweet honey gone

ume- apricot blossoms

withered winter songs
our love bloomed at harvest moon
soon the morning chill

frosted emotions
fire warming the night chill
lullaby slumber

thoughts swept in chaos
the stars surrender to sun
lanterns have died now

blow dandelions
field of cold scattered
wishes a heart full of hope

bright hues still linger
kaleidoscope reflecting
peace from a distance

icy green forest
droplets collide into mud
in the dark of night

dandelion fluff
a breezy dance of wild weeds
scattering wishes

a purple wild haze
labyrinth of emotions
slowly fading now

curved cotton dreams fall
a view of a starry night
the moonlight hiding

trapped in our bubble
dancing in a sea of pain
exhaling to drown

frozen pinecone rise
greetings to the melted
snow sun in horizon

our shipwreck capsized
wild stark savage crow lurking
hyenas sly snark

glistening droplets
crimson rosebud opening
winter melted quick

memories fading
only darkest pain persists
bloody tears on page

waves on sandy shore
closer yet further away
pick up pretty shells

cast in ocean deep
yesterday you still loved me
memories buried

gentle with my heart
oh future lover of mine
fragile dreams of love

I have a cynical soul
and a romantic heartbeat

a sakura breeze
hold this dreaded pain
for me waterfall of tears

Sakura - Cherry blossom

cold dark words uttered
my veins frozen to your touch
disconnected souls

my cold lips trembling
confusion of rejection
icy emotions

night turns to yellow
sunflower greetings at morn
lonely tears smudged cheek

I watched him say bye
with every cold distant
word quietly faded

burning love letters
I cry because you mattered
crashing silently

agonizing heart
lonely unbearable thoughts
dull three letter words

grey dark skies above
speckled azure of hope now
because you live there

thoughts and memories
as the bright night light expands
I await the moon

through paths of pink sakura
voice echos forevermore

I need you to rest
he tears streaming down my face
do not let me lose

count your great blessings
for in the blink of an eye
it can fade away

moments of laughter
memory of hurt and pain
rose petals at dawn

lingering snowfall
muddy road where nothing grow
heavy thunderclouds

windy hazy dusk
tranquility of moonlight
stormy horizon

soul no longer seek
I now have a breeze of hope
your memory lives

glorious new dawn
birds chirping for attention
still asleep with moon

an amber nightfall
my heart full of pensive
thoughts dusk to dawn feelings

a new dawn today
unconditional love gone
reflecting love now

hold you in my heart
forevermore love to hold
at dusk I will weep

only memory
seeking your face every day
only lonely thoughts

a low hazy moon
the night sounds speak to my sou
awaiting morn' clouds

path of fallen leaves
irds in flight before storm clouds
no sunny skies here

lazy day ponder
memories of you linger
memories fading

rain falling softly
pitter patter on window
dreamingly sleepy

a breath of winter
chill in my veins icy road
traveled since the dawn

don't live in the past you
don't live there anymore
bright new beginnings

the calm of sunset
unwillingly surrender
an evening solace

icy heart of snow
dancing in yesterday's rain
tears embrace my soul

the first dawn shining
glowing amber horizons
cosmos dancing slow

the moon my shadow
hiding my darkness within
a new dawn arise

tranquil sounds tonight
mesmerized and ancient thoughts
a new dawn of hope

a plum blossom greets
infinite beauty in morn'
while birds sit and wait

a sunflower smile
on this windy sunny day
with hope of some rain

pretty butterfly
contemplating in the sun
waiting for the rain

as the night darkens
lonely heart weeps at stars
the sun smiled brightly

flower petals dance
brightest colorful greetings
a storm full of dust

leaves falling so slow
every white petal muddy
evergreen grasslands

windy jasmine breeze
hopes of forever whispered
silent tear ~ escape

embrace each moment
with tender thoughts and your
soul bleeding heart on page

covered icy snow
the pastel pink sakura
a thick blanket folds

my voice of love speaks
waiting for your soul
seeking find me under stars

full moon between clouds
the darkness all around me
awaiting the sun

a silent night sky sound
of bagpipes feintly heard
amazing grace ~Pray

amber leaves falling
a path to new beginnings
breathe in the morn' breeze

I'm dancing in hope
while watching amber
sunsets the starry sky greets

foggy magic morn'
a reflection to breathe
in hope and love collide

sun igniting day
a mineral aftertaste
soft waves shimmering

I'm alone again
you made your choice just for you
look to sakura

frozen statue now
no dancing dandelion
an elusive warmth

sunflowers watching
starving tiny insects feast
on yesterday's weeds

a lilac blanket
a peaceful embrace of calm
perfect harmony

forlorn memories
dark breezy cold winter's night
roaring crackling blaze

grey clouds hanging low
foamy waves crashing faster
an empty seashell

view from my window
wind weaving and clouds
darkened silenced by thunder

sakura petals
earth awaiting your caress
soft cold rain drizzling

sunset lullaby
hues of amber and crimson
a peaceful slumber

pensive winter thoughts
japanese instruments play
soul yearn to be free

soaking up soul words
all seventeen syllables
breathing exhaling

your soul shines brightly
breath of sakura blossoms
breathing in and out

dramatic painful
heartache at the midnight moon
turn at the crossroad

lonely butterfly
searching now, forevermore
rest along the way

feel the breeze within
inhale sakura blessings
take the soul journey

rushing through my days
yearning for my dark solace
to nourish my soul

within syllables
Nozomu is what I have
hope forevermore

Nozomu - Hope

Aisuru, love live
be awakened with true
love soul everlasting

Aisuru- to cherish

only speak your truth
do not relate to darkness
your soul breathes again

much has changed for me
lonely but not alone now
and hope still lingers

tranquil and peaceful
a river of memories
heaven reflected

lanterns burning bright
breathtaking Hirosaki
Sakura backdrop

boats rowing slowly
fishing under the moonlight
crickets sing til dawn

meadows of blossoms
the beauty of tiny buds
Hanami at dawn

beautiful autumn
rusty leaves falling slowly
soak up life's moments

moonlit covered path
distant temple bell echoes
gifts to behold now

glistening sunrise
white mountain snow horizen
melted memories

enchanted temple
cold frosted emerald path
sitting Buddha greets

scarlet petals fall
muddy ground covered with gifts
nature's earth nourished

ancient syllables
the language of peace
our tranquility

skies of amber dusk
halfmoon hiding between clouds
stars greeting lovers

summer rainfall dawn
glowing colorful rainbow
traces across my heart

bright morning sunrise
butterflies feast on peta
ls sipping black coffee

I wake up to see beauty
fall asleep with memories

dark storm clouds floating
an old well granting wishes
as the fireflies dance

the break of sunrise
romantic Sakura path
blossoms blossoming

awakening love
gratitude surrounding now
moonlight greets dawns light

matcha moonlight drink
as the stars glistens brightly
love forevermore

through my Haiku soul
four seasons in a day lived
a life full of change

silently gazing
pensively dreaming, reflect
blossoms in full bloom

calm of new morning
scented breeze of sakura
tranquility felt

ever-changing soul
sun fire at the dawn clouds
mirror of my thoughts

footsteps on dew green
icicles of snow melting
hot matcha steeping

dark silent night sky
owl hoot in the distant oak
restless thoughts looming

delicate pastel
dancing to the ground with wind
life changes swiftly

amber crunching leaves
winter will be over soon
soul embraced nature

silver glow river
colorful butterflies dance
poppies swaying slow

strolling through meadow
gentle hush masked the forest
trees awaiting touch of spring

banished winter chill
thin light through puffy white cloud
birds feast first candy

sand between my toes
foamy waves, footprints vanished
collecting pearl shells

wisteria bloom
lavender sway, lazy wind
butterfly medley

sunset silhouettes
shadows in garden of peace
bamboo scented breeze

hibutsu, Buddha
sacred temple pilgrimage
gain enlightenment

Nakama~our souls
forevermore connected
banded so closely

Awayuki~ligt snow
soft misty snow blanket fall
icy chilled winter

Momo-no-Sekku
festival of peach blossoms
pretty pink petals

ocean waves linger
darkest midnight skies above
thunder whispering

chilled blue undertone
icy breeze curling around
white sun-kissed blossoms

Hatsuhi~first sun
beginnings, forgotten old
tangerine sun glow

syllables heal souls
through a peaceful garden path
pastel sakura

a lazy full moon
wandering around the pond
autumn amber dusk

on the temple bell
await rainbow butterfly
fresh sakura breeze

dry sage leaves burning
cleansing old sin, end bad vibes
fragrant smokey air

graced by a bright moon
blazing sun in deep slumber
stars above Tori

first summer rainfall
autumn wind vanished again
chanting and dancing

dewdrops glistening
icy winter storm lurking
crow in the distance

soaking up soul words
all seventeen syllables
breathing, exhaling

soft lilac blanket
a peaceful embrace of calm
perfect harmony

contemplate your thoughts
the heat of a summers night
a path of hope felt

Haiku, my first love
syllable by syllable
soaked in nature's gift

sacred reflecting
spiritual peace and love
unconditional

inhale Sakura
exhale syllables daily
fragrant poetic

a silent night sky
distant sound of temple bell
the stars shining bright

breathing in and out
allow slow breathing pattern
breeze rustling across

wispy clouds swaying
standing on the river's edge
an earthy' morn breeze

a calm mind within
encapsulated in peace
devine energy

ocean blue tranquility
still, without any chaos

Mii-dera found
survived more raging fires
poured sacred knowledge

butterflies flirting
a path of soft Sakura
light raindrops drizzle

Shiogoshi pine
shiny droplets of moonlight
fallen and scattered

slow waves of blossoms
a sunny day cascading
shifted direction

tiny beads of dew
caress Sakura at morn
temple bells echo

ancient temple grounds
wrapped in early morning haze
mountain and garden

whisper silently
chanting to Lotus Sutra
national treasure

Matsuo Basho lived
Iga, birthplace of master
inhale syllables

reading and learning
some saw you as poor peasant
my Haiku mentor

a full autumn moon
resting in the darkest sky
mountains and rivers

syllables heal souls
through a peaceful garden path
pastel Sakura

unconditional
souls feel daily syllables
together always

footprints in the sand
ocean waves crash high and low
happy seagull greets

peace and silence evermore
a whispering wind echos

keep peace in your soul
even through chaos, be still
strive for your calmness

in a summer haze
dance to the song in your heart
thunder storm arise

soft meditation
truth between the path to soul
unfolding lotus

amber leaves falling
a path to new beginnings
breathe in the 'morn breeze

an endless winter
a fireplace to ruminate
ancient thoughts linger

write with your soul and
imagine a world full of
Sakura blossoms

reflecting deeply
the temple bell sounds echo
time for quiet rest

moon resting among
swaying Sakura petals
chanting faintly heard

an evening mantra
allow petals to bloom and
inhale fragrant gifts

we share hurt and pain
inhale the beauty of words
heal through syllables

ocean waves splashing
the sun embracing my soul
healing and breathing

More books by Alta H Haffner

alta@sakurabookpublishing.com

www.ingramcontent.com/pod-product-compliance
Lightning Source LLC
Chambersburg PA
CBHW051559010526
44118CB00023B/2754